FINDING THE UNEXPECTED

SEARCHING UTIAN FAMILY ROOTS IN LITHUANIA

OTHER BOOKS BY WULF UTIAN

The Menopause Manual – A Woman's Guide to the Menopause (MTP Press, Lancaster, UK, 1978)

Menopause in Modern Perspective (Appleton-Century-Crofts, 1980)

Your Middle Years: A Doctor's Guide for Today's Woman (Appleton-Century-Crofts, 1980)

The Premenstrual Syndrome, Pieter van Keep, Wulf H. Utian (MTP Press, Lancaster, UK, 1981)

The Controversial Climacteric, Pieter van Keep, Wulf H. Utian, Alex Vermuelen (MTP Press, Lancaster, UK, 1982)

Multidisciplinary Perspectives on Menopause, Marcha Flint, Fredi Kronenberg, Wulf Utian (*Annals of the New York Academy of Sciences,* Volume 592, June 13, 1990)

Managing Your Menopause, Wulf H. Utian, Ruth S. Jacobowitz (Prentice Hall Press, New York, NY, 1990)

The Menopause and Hormonal Replacement Therapy: Facts and Controversies, Regine Sitruk-Ware, Wulf H. Utian (Marcel Dekker, New York, NY, 1991)

THE UTIAN STRATEGY: is this my problem or is this your problem? (Utian Press, Beachwood, Ohio, 2010)

CHANGE YOUR MENOPAUSE. Why one size does not fit all. (Utian Press, Beachwood, Ohio, 2011)

FINDING THE UNEXPECTED

SEARCHING UTIAN FAMILY ROOTS IN LITHUANIA

SEPTEMBER 1-7, 2014

WULF H. UTIAN

UTIAN PRESS
Beachwood, Ohio

Copyright © 2014 by Wulf H. Utian

UTIAN PRESS
Beachwood, Ohio
www.utianllc.com

First Edition, October 2014

ISBN 978-0-9828457-6-9 (print edition)

ISBN 978-0-9828457-7-6 (eBook edition)

DEDICATION

"From 1881 to 1914, more than 2.5 million Jews migrated from Eastern Europe, i.e. some 80,000 each year... A further distinguishing feature of Jewish migration was that from the outset it displayed clearly ideological tendencies. A considerable number of the younger immigrants, members of the intelligentsia, were motivated not only by the desire to find a new refuge or a place in which there were greater chances of success; their departure constituted a protest against the discrimination and injustices they had suffered in their old homes and reflected their ardent desire for a place in which they could live independent and free lives."

From: *A History of the Jewish People*, Edited by H.H. Ben-Sasson
Harvard University Press, 1976.

This short book is a record of a search for information about
two young brothers who were part of that migration.

I dedicate this book to the memory of my father and my uncle,
Harry (Hersh) Mendel Utian, and Boris (Ber) Utian,
and to their families whose lives were so cruelly ended.

ACKNOWLEDGEMENTS

I thank my brother Martin Utian of Vancouver, Canada, for his deep involvement in the major database searches, and his cheerful willingness to help with his computer skills in bringing this manuscript to finality.

I thank my sister Glika Kiselstein of Tel Aviv, Israel, for searching old photographs.

I thank my friend Hilly Nackan of Johannesburg, South Africa, for giving me a copy of his uncle's map, and for the genealogical contacts.

IT ALL BEGAN WITH A HAND-DRAWN MAP...

THE TOWN AND RESIDENTS OF PASVAL circa 1926

DRAWN BY
ABRAM NACKAN.

IT ALL BEGAN WITH A HAND-DRAWN MAP
PASVAL, CIRCA 1926, BY ABRAM NACKAN

BACKGROUND

This is a story about the past coming back to reinforce the present. It all began with a hand-drawn map of a small village in Lithuania, near Vilna.

There is much to be said in favor about remembering who you are and where you came from. The first rule is to keep in touch or reconnect with friends from the past.

The hand drawn map of Pasval, circa 1926, best supports this philosophy. For some years, my wife Moira and I on our irregular visits to Johannesburg have been contacting old friends and trying to reconnect. About 3 years ago, I phoned Hilly Nackan, and invited him to join Moira and me for breakfast. We had not seen each other for well over 35 years. Hilly was not only a good childhood friend, but our fathers', Harry (Mendel) Utian and Zelik Nackan, were 'landsmen' from the small shtetl of Pasval in Lithuania. His father, his uncle, and my father and his brother Boris (Ber) had emigrated from Lithuania to South Africa in the early 1900's.

Hilly arrived with a briefcase containing a treasure trove of old documents and a copy of a personal memoir he was working on. Included was a map his uncle Abram Nackan had drawn for him some years ago before he passed away. The map was unique in that every house was numbered and the occupants listed down the side of the document.

The following year in Johannesburg I arranged an evening with my Utian cousins, Hessel, Ruth and Gordon, to share the map and try and delve into the history of Harry and Boris. We felt the only way to get to know more was to travel to Pasval. But it took yet another year until Kevin, Gordon's eldest son, decided to gift his father a special birthday present of a trip to Lithuania that we all began to seriously plan and eventually undertake an 'on the ground' search of the roots of the Utians.

With the Internet and modern communications there is an incredible amount of information out there for the searching. Fortunately my brother Martin is really computer smart, and before we left uncovered a wealth of background information. Through Jewishgen and other websites he traced Utian's in Vilna back to around 1768, and Utiansky's in Pasval from the 1800's.

Harry had been loathe to discuss his past. What we do know comes from what he told my mother Ettie (Ethel), nee Nay (Narunsky), and a surprise bonus in a school project she helped Martin's son Dean with on the early life of Harry Utian. Since much of this was hearsay, clearly there was a need to delve deeper and confirm.

Boris left Pasval around 1918, and Harry followed just over 2 years later. Martin found the passenger list from the Union Castle Line ship, the Saxon, on which Harry, identified as a student aged 16, departed on December 9, 1921, from Southampton to Cape Town, and the address of where he had been living in London. The address of 27 Leman Street was found to be the Jews Temporary Shelter.

The following is an abbreviation of information obtained from the South African Jewish Genealogy SA-SIG:

"The 'Poor Jews Temporary Shelter' functioned in London in the nineteenth and twentieth centuries. Probably the best known was in Leman Street in London's East End. Migrants passed through the Shelter en route to South Africa, America and other places. Many of the Jews embarked initially at the ports of Libau and were transported on small cargo boats under crude conditions to England. Many came first to Grimsby or London and were taken to the Poor Jews' Temporary Shelter in Leman Street in the East End of London. Some assistance in the form of board, lodging, medical advice and advice on travel was given by the Shelter. In one year from Nov 1902, 3600 out of 4500 inmates went on to South Africa. From here most went on the Union Castle Line to the Cape. In 1902 the fare was £10.10.0 (ten guineas)- more than the fare to America."

What happened immediately on Harry's arrival in South Africa is unclear, where he lived, how he went to school, and what triggered his interest to become a manufacturing jeweler and diamond expert. He eventually became one of the founding members of the South African Diamond Exchange.

Also unclear was what had happened to the family remaining behind in Pasval. By 1963 we knew that his brother Zelik and sister Beila had survived and were living in Moscow. The belief was that the rest had been rounded up by the Germans and transported to Auschwitz. In fact with this assumption, my sister Glika had recorded their names at Yad Vashem as having perished in Auschwitz.

Now we were to find out the truth...

THE JEWS TEMPORARY SHELTER, 27 LEMAN SREET, LONDON

No. of Ship "Saxon"

Date of Departure 9th December 1921.

Steamship Line Union-Castle Mail S.S. Coy Ltd

Where Bound South Africa

NAMES AND DESCRIPTIONS OF **ALIEN** PASSENGERS EMBARKED AT THE PORT OF Southampton

B.—NON-TRANSMIGRANTS, that is Alien Passengers other than those included under A.

Third Class Contd.

Names of Passengers	Last Address in the United Kingdom	Port at which Passengers have contracted to land	Profession, Occupation or Calling	Country of which Citizen or Subject	Country of Intended Future Permanent Residence
Brought forward					
Wafner Mr Nahman / Miss Dina	82 Leman St. E.	Capetown	Dealer / Clerk	Poland	S. Africa
Abram Mr Chaim	82 Leman St. E.		Labourer	Lithuania	
Bruno Mr Michel / Mr Pietro	136 Bishopsgate, London E.		Baker / Miner	Italy	Rhodesia
Druker Mrs Mary / Mr Zadok / Miss Sheine / Master Nachman / Miss Pesse	82 Leman St. E.		Nil	Lithuania	S. Africa
Kaplan Mr Joseph			Druggist		
Kaimowitz Mrs Bella / Master Jakhal / Isaak / Max	24 Norton Folgate E.		Nil / Bookbinder / Nil	Poland	
Levin Mrs Mary / Mast. Hirsch / Miss Basse / Master Leijer / Mashe	82 Leman St. E.			Lithuania	
Moscowitz Mr Mordke		Natal	Student	Poland	
Oliv Mr Carl Gustav	30 W. India Dock Rd E.		Carpenter	Sweden	
Slonimsky Mr Simon		Capetown	Watchmaker	Lithuania	
Scheiman Mr Melech	82 Leman St. E.			Latvia	
Saut Miss Sora / Miss Ida			Nil	Lithuania	
Friedland Mr Jacob	82 Leman St. E.		Barber		
Orkin Miss Micha			Cashier		
Uliansky Mr Mendel	82 Leman St.		Student		
Saho Mr Berel	E.		Tinsmith		
Resnik Mr Berel			Butcher		
Beskow Mr Chaim	do.		Merchant		
Ferm Mr Henij / Mrs Schenna	90 Union Castle Line, London		Nil	Holland	

C. No. 440 C.

Images reproduced by courtesy of The National Archives, London, England. www.nationalarchives.gov.uk
Digitised by www.1837online.com

The first known photograph of Boris and Harry in Johannesburg, South Africa, was taken around 1922 at the Wilds, a nature reservation just outside of downtown. What strikes me most is the body language of two young men, fresh in a new country, seemingly bursting with confidence.

Boris at about 24   Harry at about age 17
Fannie Treisman, a cousin

AT THE JOHANNESBURG WILDS APPROXIMATELY 1922

Before departing from Cleveland I was able, through contacts, to get the Director of the Lithuanian Archives in Vilnius to undertake background research and have documents available for us to review when we got there.

Our objectives in Lithuania were to find documentary evidence on the Utians of Vilnius and Utianskys of Pasval, to confirm whether the structure still standing in Pasval was the home of our grandfather Shmuel Mordechai Utiansky, and uncover any other information of their lives and their tragic ending.

The only direct documentary evidence I had for Harry on communication with his Pasval family was a 1938 letter from his brother Abraham, with contributions from his half-sister Chaya Sara, and his father, dated 1938, congratulating Harry and Ethel on their marriage, also enclosing a photograph. This confirmed that Shmuel Mordechai was alive in 1938.

ELIEZER   CHAYA SARALA   ABRAHAM

CHANA   SHMUEL MORDECHAI

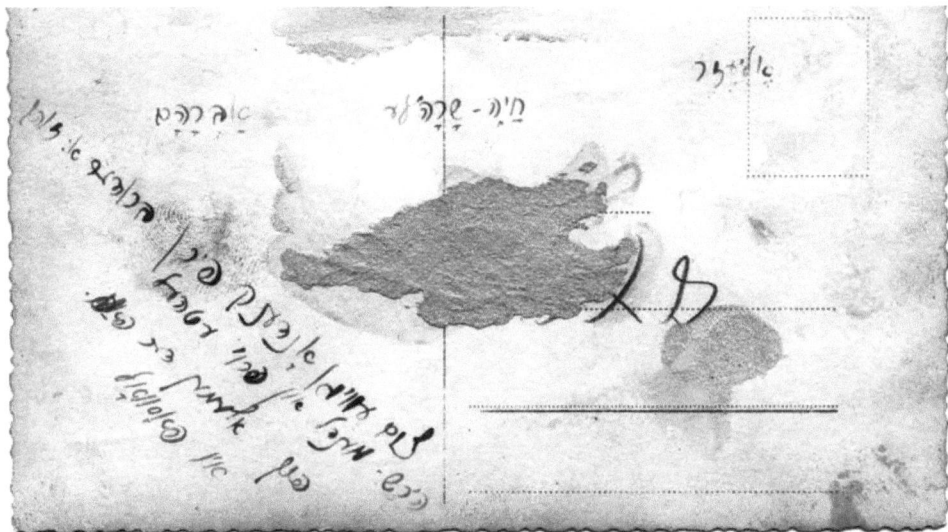

THE REVERSE: FOR EVERLASTING MEMORY FOR OUR BROTHER AND SON, HERSH MENDEL AND WIFE ETHEL.
FROM EVERYBODY HERE IN PASVAL

It is almost certain that the photo was enclosed with the letter, with three of the five in the photo having written the letter. Also intriguing is Abraham and Chaya Sara's good use of English, and the copper plate handwriting. The 1938 letter is a vibrant memory of real people who seemed just vague phantoms in our family history.

The letter is shown below. The photos of Harry and Ethel (Ettie) on their wedding day in 1938 to me are also striking for the magnificence of their outfits. They must have been a very handsome couple. A cousin, Henry Treisman, who had become the leading wedding photographer at that time in Johannesburg, took the photographs.

Vytauto Did. aikště (Place o name
Vytautas Tre By) 19A
Pasvalys, Lietuva-Lithuania,
22th May 1938.

My dearest sisther a brother,

    At first I please you, lovest sisther, excuse me for the unright to call you sisther. But I feel, that from the time my lovest brother Harry married a nice wonderful sisther to ours all cames. And indeed a loving sisther-heart you have, my best sisther! And I press as a really brother your hands. sisther and brother, to your happier marriage, that shall be the gate door into your both famous happiness. With best wishes of really love we incorpore you loving sisther in circus of our family a best relations, as a really daughter to father a mother and a sisther to our all. We admire seeing such a nice human we became in our family with thy marriage with they-(a also our certainly) - heartslove, dear brother.

    Your dear letter, sisther, I read with much or the most pleasure I have, and how much I could I tola all your loving words in Jewish to father a mother. They are very happy and glad into tears to hear something dearest from you sisther, may it be in English, or you brother mouths, to see you on your photo's and certainly to see your own signatures on the paper. God give to see you all ou best health and happy, because we mind your happiness is our and therefore we all like to see you all as ours in overseas

as nice a best feeling with really human heart men one
to other, while to the ill and old-grey our all loving
father a mother it will be the best physic to see your
letter as a dearest and lovest thing and to hear from
you all the best always.

     I close my letter, there I enclosed father a
mother best wishes etc, with best hopes to see you all really
happy. God give by the time the letter reaches you
our best collective wishes to you all will be to your best
health.

     In waiting your dearest words, sister a brother,
I signature   your lovest brother
                               Abraham

My best wishes to you all, — sister and
brother, from you — loving sister
                          Chaya - tara

LETTER FROM PASVAL, DATED MAY 22, 1938

11

1938 WEDDING PHOTOS OF
HARRY UTIAN AND ETHEL NAY
(NARUNSKY)

On Sunday August 31, 2014, four Utians, Brett, Gordon, Kevin, and Daryn, left Johannesburg for Vilnius via Frankfurt, and I left New York via Stockholm.

None of us knew really what to expect. And none of us could have anticipated what we were about to uncover, the joy and sadness we would share, and the bonding of five Utians as we set off in search of our roots.

The odyssey is presented as it happened, because new and unexpected findings kept cropping up, and doubtless more will be discovered long after this document is written.

MONDAY, SEPTEMBER 1.
ARRIVAL IN LITHUANIA

Vilnius from the air looks poor. First impressions seem to be confirmed in the drive from the airport, until one arrives in historic Old Town Vilnius. Then one is quite surprised. Expect the worst and hope for the best is how one can describe this experience. Historic Old Town Vilnius is, quite rightly, a world heritage site for historic preservation. There is a wonderful mix of old–world classical and Baroque architecture. The buildings are in great shape, the cobbled roads remarkably clean, and everyone seems to be thin, content and mostly very attractive. Dress is western but smart casual, and the many tall, invariably blond women are very stylishly dressed. Many top brand stores are here, but tourist traffic seems limited. Beyond the old town new high rise buildings, shopping centers, and housing complexes are ample evidence of an expanding middle class.

COBBLESTONED PILIES STREET, OLD TOWN

VILNIUS CATHEDRAL

UNIVERSITY OF VILNIUS (FOUNDED 1568)
AND LITTERA BOOKSHOP

TUESDAY, SEPTEMBER 2.
JEWISH VILNIUS

For the first time in many decades there were 5 adult male Utians in Vilnius. My cousin Gordon, his two sons Kevin and Daryn, and my son Brett met our Jewish guide Svetlana Shtarkman in the lobby of the Radisson Blu Hotel. The latter is a renovated old Astoria Hotel, built in 1901, with a well-matched new wing in the heart of Old Town.

DARYN   KEVIN   GORDON WULF BRETT

.......................AND THE VILNA GAON

Our objectives for today were to get an introduction to Jewish Vilna, what was and what is, and especially to try and trace references to the Utians of Vilna.

The hours-long walk through the original ghettos of Vilnius took us along the old cobbled streets to the site of the teachings of the Vilna Gaon, to a Jewish Information Center, the latter with reconstructed hidden underground bunkers where Jews hid during times of danger, and many references to Jewish activity. We also came across the site of the most active bohemian café of avant-garde Jewish Vilna, Velfkeh's (Wolfie's) run by Wolfie Ussian, described as "...one of Vilna's famous institutions. Here Vilna's Yiddish writers, actors, and intellectuals came to eat and drink, to entertain their out-of-town guests, to celebrate festive occasions, and sometimes just to enjoy themselves." (Lucy Davidowicz, *From That Time and Place*, Norton, New York, 1989).

The only shul to survive the Germans out of nearly 140 in Lithuania is called the Choral Synagogue and it resembles in many ways the Gardens Shul in Cape Town. It was developed in 1903 by a more modern Jewish community, and named the choral because of the open galleries upstairs for women and the choir.

EXPLORING JEWISH VILNA, IN REALITY, THE SAD REMAINS
(*PRECEDING PAGE*: THE CHORAL SYNAGOGUE)

We also got an acute insight to the extent of anti-Semitism and the horrors of the wars by visiting the Jewish cemeteries. The first cemetery is completely non-existent, having been totally raised by the Nazi's. The second has only a monument built of gravestones that were collected after the collapse of the Soviet Union and Russian occupation ending in 1991, and which had been used as building materials for staircases and walkways around the city. Finally we walked the current cemetery, started in 1945 after the defeat of the Nazi's. Here exists a tomb moved by means unknown to hold the remains of the Vilna Gaon. In a far corner is the resting place for the final 200 children taken from the ghetto, and drained of their blood and de-skinned for use in medical care of German soldiers, and then hidden in a common grave.

THE SECOND JEWISH CEMETERY
GRAVESTONES THAT WERE USED FOR STAIRCASES

The most unexpected experience of the day, one we found to raise goose bumps and quite blow us away, was a visit to the Archives of Vilnius. Thanks to Hilly Nackan of Johannesburg (our fathers were both from Pasval) and a contact he gave me in Washington DC, I was able to arrange a visit ahead of time with the head of the archives, Dr. Galina Baranova. On a desk in her office she had accumulated a mountain of documents and old bound books. The latter turned out to include birth registers for Lithuania between about 1880 and 1912.

DR GALINA BARINOVA, DIRECTOR OF THE LITHUANIAN
ARCHIVES
REVEALING OUR ROOTS

I almost lost my breath when she opened the 1905 Register to the page showing my late father's entry, complete with his date of birth of May 13, 1905, the names of his parents and siblings, and even the date and names of the 2 Rabbi's who conducted his bris. Entries were in Russian on the left page and Yiddish on the opposite page. Hersh' (Harry) surname was first given as Utiansky and then deleted and amended in the same entry to Utian. We also learned that the dates until 1916 followed an Old Russian calendar, and that to get the true date of birth one needs to add 12 days. So by our current calendar, my Dad was born on May 25, 1905. We are being provided with fully validated copies of the pages and the birth certificates.

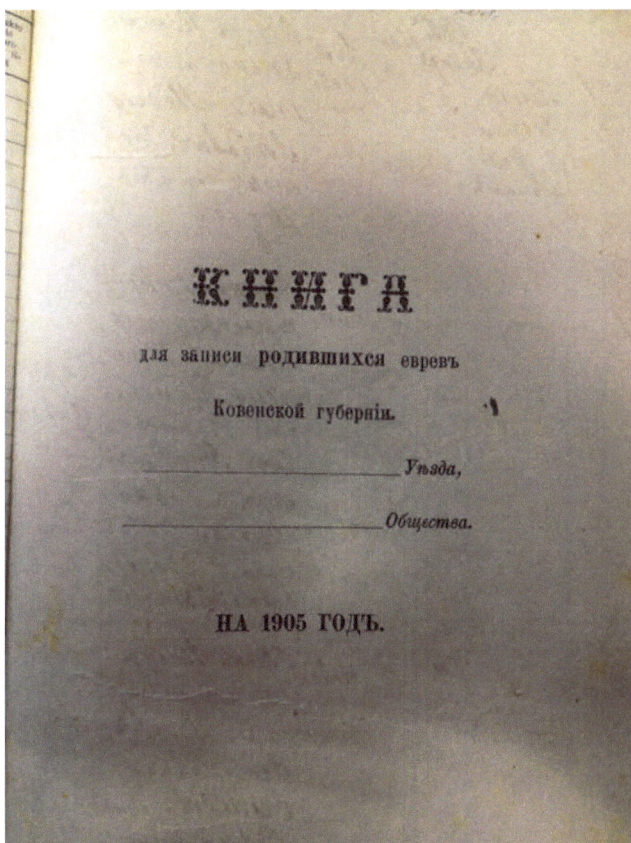

КНИГА

для записи родившихся евреъ

Ковенской губерніи.

_____ Уѣзда,

_____ Общества.

НА 1905 ГОДЪ.

LITHUANIA BIRTH REGISTER OF 1905

RECORD OF BIRTH OF HERSH (HARRY) UTIAN, MAY 13,1905

This was, in all, a very productive day, and tomorrow we leave early for Pasval (Pasvalys) to see if the house of Boris and Harry's father, Shmuel Mordechai, still exists.

WEDNESDAY, SEPTEMBER 3, 2014.
PASVAL AND VICINITY

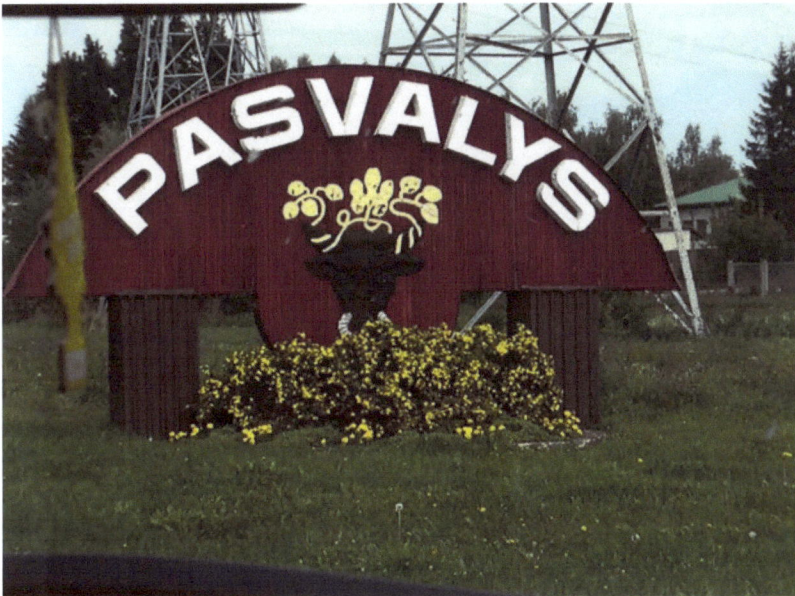

Pasval (now called Pasvalys), the birthplace of Gordon and my fathers, lies about 175 km northwest of Vilnius, reached by a remarkably good freeway. The area was part of the Pale of Settlement.

Arriving in Pasval I had always lived with the inherent understanding that my grandfather, Shmuel Mordechai Utiansky, was a Tevya-like figure living in poverty in a wooden house in a shtetl in Lithuania or Russia, as the border moved. Instead what we found was totally surprising and unexpected.

There certainly were wooden houses, the above being a nearby example, but many were really substantial structures. Most are picturesquely situated along the river, some in good shape and others in disrepair.

We parked close to the estimated site of our grandfather's home, and looked around in some confusion. Were these the homes they had lived in, and if so, which one had belonged to Shmuel Mordechai?

ARRIVING IN PASVAL
AND WERE THESE REALLY THE HOMES?

Shmuel Mordechai's first wife, my grandmother, Hesse Rochel nee Mozeson, had died on March 27, 1909, with my father less than age 4. My father, Hersh (Harry), left Pasval in 1920 at the age of 15, somehow travelled alone to London, and left for South Africa alone in 1921. Remember, we had a copy of the Union Castle Line ship's manifest showing him as a passenger, identified as a student. We have always assumed he had left because he wanted to escape conscription into the Russian army, and indeed have documentary evidence that he had been registered. Now I wonder if something else had come into play. His father remarried in 1910 to Chana nee Evin, and Harry may well have left to get away from the stepmother. Again, we have official documentation of all these dates and events.

Harry almost certainly left a wooden house situated in the most prime position of Pasval on the market square across the street from the main village church, with the river beyond. But unbeknown to him, and his brother Boris who had left for South Africa 2-3 years before, Shmuel Mordechai had prospered after the First World War as a timber merchant with his own forest and was also engaged in fuel production. Official documents show his status over these years changing from 'clerk' to 'merchant', and he is listed as such in the book Visa Lietuva of the Central Statistics Bureau of 1931. In the same records, his second wife Chana is listed under the section of businessmen as being an hotelier.

A new fire code was introduced for the central town in early 1921, so the old wooden house was demolished, and a new brick edifice built on the same site. Shmuel built a 3-story hotel with family living quarters, and office for his timber business. He continued to run the timber business, and his wife Chana ran the hotel. They are both also so identified in multiple telephone books and town catalogues, the last telephone book being that of 1940. Evidence of his prosperity is that they acquired one of the first telephones in Pasval, their telephone number being 3.

As we were exploring, the next-door neighbor, alighting from his car, asked our guide about us. Contrary to our expectations of being chased out of town with a shotgun, "5 Jews coming to reclaim property", his face lit up and he invited us into his house for morning coffee and biscuits. He turned out to be a successful businessman, running the regions' flour mills, acquired after no Jewish survivors were able to lodge a claim under the liberal laws for Jews of the current government.

GIEDRIUS UZDAVINYS, SVETLANA, AND DARYN
IN THE HOUSE NEXT DOOR

Through our guide's interpretation he and his charming wife told us that the town had heard of our upcoming visit through news of the research Svetlana had undertaken prior to our arrival. They were delighted to welcome us, and the head of the local museum was eagerly waiting to see us.

THE VIEW FROM THE WINDOW NEXT DOOR,
VIRTUALLY IDENTICAL TO THE VIEW THE UTIAN FAMILY WOULD
HAVE HAD, LOOKING AT THE CHURCH AND THE RIVER BEYOND

At the museum we were again presented with documentary evidence of the status of our grandfather and his second wife, as well as shown old photos of the houses on the market square facing the church somewhere in the early 1930's. Our grandfather's property was easily identified. It also seems that Jews and non-Jews got on relatively well in the Lithuanian shtetls, at least symbiotically, before about 1938, the former being merchants, bankers and scholars, and the latter working in agriculture.

THE PASVALYS MUSEUM DIRECTOR HELPS US PINPOINT
THE EXACT HOME OF SHMUEL MORDECHAI

SHMUEL, LISTED AS SAMUELIS UTIANSKIS,
IN PHONE BOOKS OF THE 1930'S AND 1940

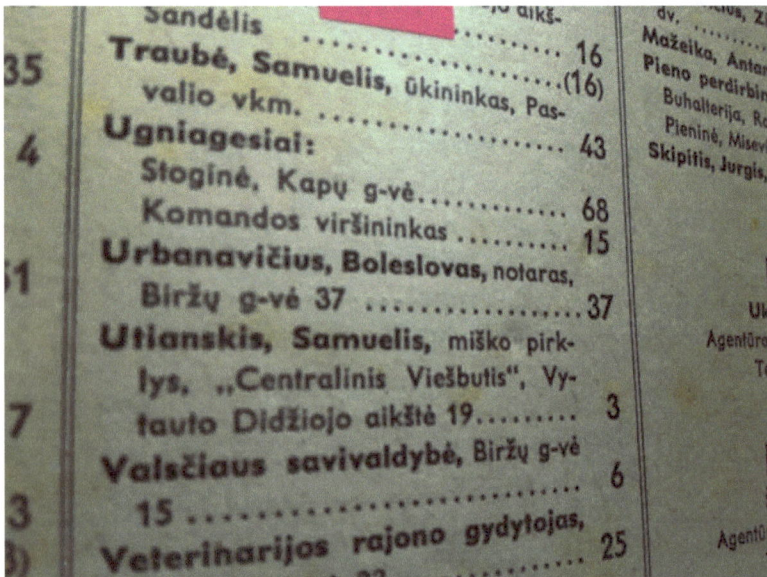

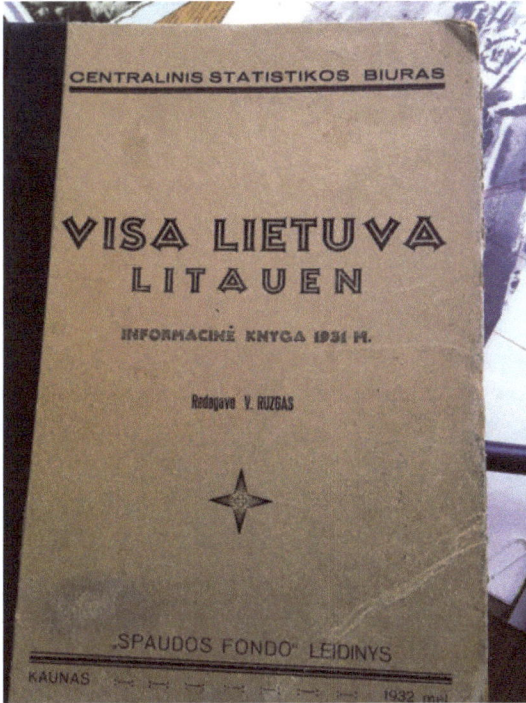

…AND CHANA, LISTED UNDER THE HOTEL CATEGORY, ALSO APPEARS IN BUSINESS DIRECTORIES

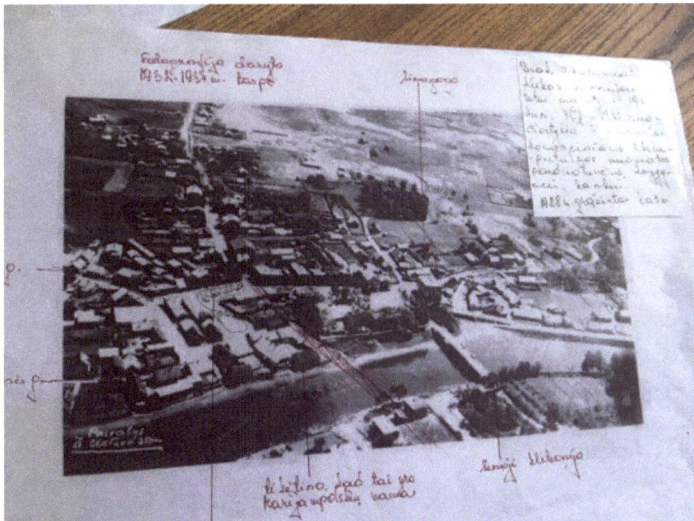

Armed with our new information, we returned to the market square, and found the house/hotel/business office of Shmuel Mordechai, and family.

YES, THIS ENTIRE BUILDING WAS THE FAMILY HOME

Sadly, I doubt Boris and Harry ever knew any details of the more affluent life of their father and remaining siblings, nor indeed do I have reason to believe his father had much knowledge about what had happened to the 2 boys as there is little evidence of their communicating between 1921 and 1940. We do have that letter from his brother Abraham, dated 1938, congratulating Harry on his marriage to my mother Ethel (Ettie), Nee Nay (Narunsky), with the added note in Yiddish from his father. This is also the further evidence that Shmuel Mordechai was alive in 1938, and the telephone books, as above, seem to prove for even longer.

The occupants upstairs were not home, but the ground floor had been converted into a quaint restaurant and bar, and 5 Utians drank a toast to their tragically departed family from inside the family home.

THE UTIANS ARE BACK!
DRINKING A TOAST TO OUR DEPARTED FAMILY

BRETT IN THE
ENTRANCE HALL OF
THE HOME, AND BOTH
OF US AT THE FRONT
DOOR BELOW

A walkabout of the village showed what a rich life the Jewish community of Pasval must have enjoyed. We saw the remains of the shul, an unusually large brick and concrete structure, now in use as a hardware and building supply store. Similarly there was a solid mikvah.

A MISERABLE END TO A GLORIOUS SHUL

THE MIKVAH AND THE REMAINS OF THE JEWISH CEMETERY

The comfortable Pasval life came to an abrupt end after June 26, 1941. From about 1938 "German Tourists' had began appearing in Lithuania laying seeds for rabid anti-Semitism. On June 26, 1941, the German army swept through Pasval, stopping for little more than a couple of hours in the shtetl. They told the locals that they were free and independent of the tyranny of Russia, and the property of the 'Bolshevist' Jews was theirs for the taking, provided they got rid of the Jews.

The Town Councilors of the shtetls were given 3 options to eliminate the Jews, to expel them, to put them into labor camps, or to exterminate them. In Pasval the Town Council voted for extermination, and somewhere between June 26 and early September, the Jews were taken deep into a forest at Zadeikiuose, shot, and buried in a mass grave.

One survivor was able to identify the site after the Nazis were defeated. The same story was repeated in shtetls across Lithuania, with locals, not Germans, being the killers. This occurred before there were ghettos in Vilna or other big cities. In 1941 there were about 1600 Jews living in Pasvalys. With few exceptions, all were murdered at Zadeikiuose.

We visited the Pasval Jewish cemetery where only a handful of broken gravestones still exist, and where our grandmother and other family members who had passed away in the years before the massacre are buried in unidentified graves.

We then drove along a dirt track deep into the forest to the killing site at Zadeikiuose where doubtless Shmuel and his family were wiped out. We walked the forest and stood by the mass graves where they were killed. It is a haunting experience.

THE KILLING FIELDS AND GRAVE AT ZADEIKIUOSE

We do not know exactly what happened to the siblings and stepsiblings, how many had remained in Pasval and were there for the genocide of 1941. Certainly Zelik, born February 7, 1893, and Beila, born May 2, 1896, eventually got to Moscow, where my parents and I met with them in 1964. Nechemia, born September 12, 1894, ran away leaving no trace. Abraham, born July 3, 1897, was still in Vilna until 1938, as evidenced by the letter mentioned above, and so almost certainly perished in 1941 with his father, stepmother and sister Taube Glika, born February 11, 1900, and step-siblings, and they were buried in the mass grave.

That evening the Lithuanian Ambassador to Israel and South Africa, Darius Degutis, visited us at our hotel and confirmed this ugly history. He told us that no European country has passed stronger laws to teach this awful history to the next generation than Lithuania. He also explained that Lithuania was the strongest pro-Israel country in Europe, particularly as they equated Israel's hostile neighbors with Putin as their enemy right on their doorstep. My sleep that night was troubled; yet elated by what we had discovered about the family and their home.

LITHUANIAN MARKERS TO KILLING AND HOLOCAUST SITES

THURSDAY, SEPTEMBER 4.
THE KILLING FIELDS OF PANEREI FOREST,
AND MORE JEWISH VILNIUS

An early start took us about 20 minutes out of Vilnius to deep into the forest at Paneriai. This was the spot to which the Jews of Vilna and some surrounding areas were brought and exterminated. The area had been developed by the Soviets as a potential fuel depot, and deep pits had been dug to hold fuel tanks. Before completion the Germans rolled in and the Soviets fled. Those few that did not get away were the first to be executed here.

After about September of 1941 the Germans went into full swing with their extermination project against the Jews, aided and abetted by many Lithuanian assistants. As we walked the killing pits it was difficult to understand, comprehend, or get one's mind around the enormity of the genocide.

One pit was a drop off point for the Jews to leave their belongings and shed their clothes. Later in the day, after the killings, local inhabitants were invited to come and help themselves to the spoils. We stood near a pit where Germans, in order to save bullets, had taken children by the legs and smashed their heads against trees.

In 1944, as the Russians approached, the Germans began to panic about their vile deeds being discovered. We overlooked a large pit where captives had been kept chained in the pit digging up bodies to burn, and the bones to be ground into powder. In one pit 15 of these captives had dug a tunnel out the side over a period of 2 months and about 11 managed to escape and join the partisans in the woods. Their horrific memories are recorded in the nearby museum.

We walked in this forest of horror, silent, shocked, and in disbelief that so-called civilized people could commit such atrocities.

THE KILLING FIELDS
AT PANEREI

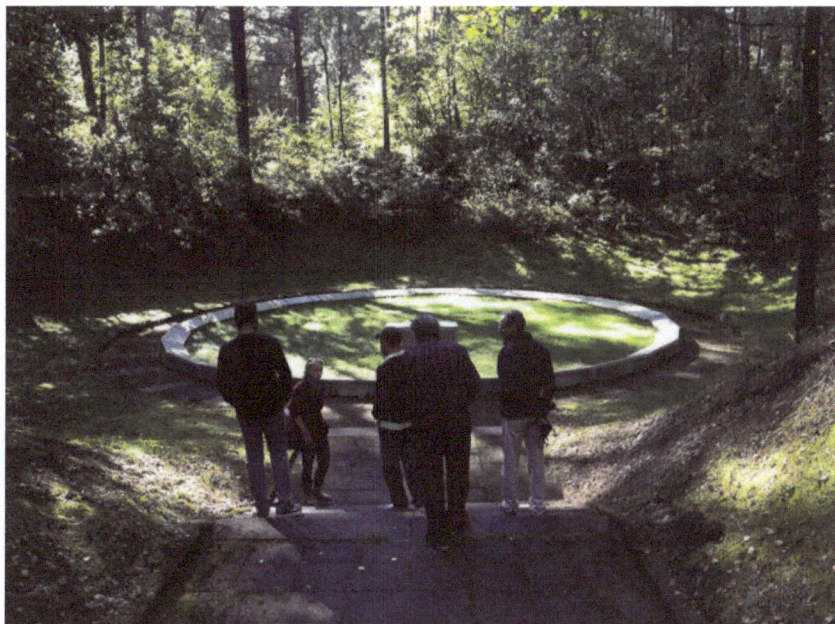

THERE IS NO WAY TO UNDERSTAND WHAT HAPPENED AT PANEREI

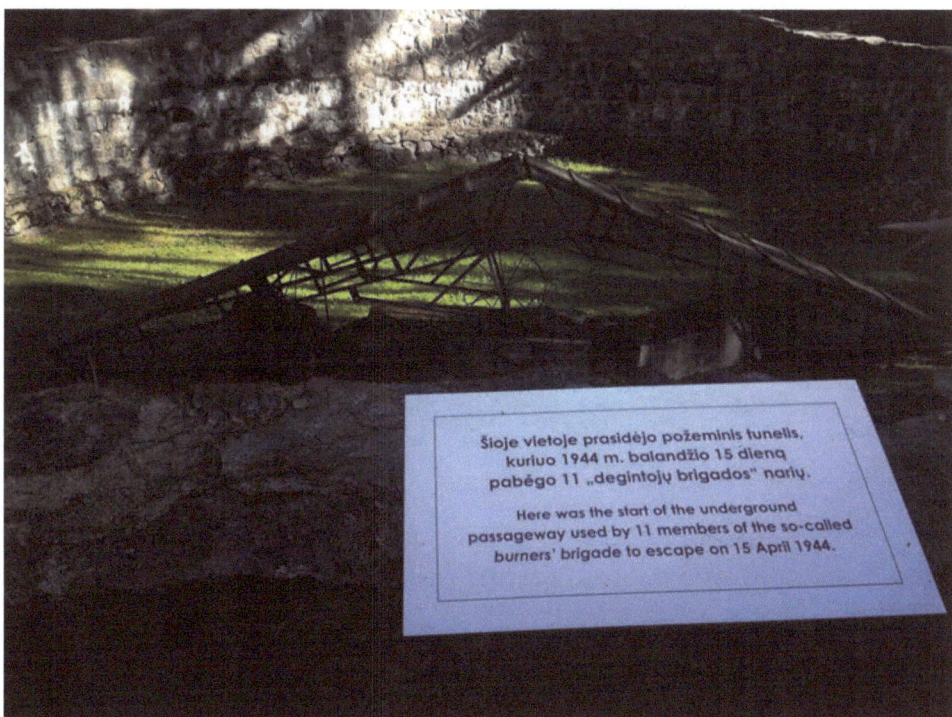

Šioje vietoje prasidėjo požeminis tunelis,
kuriuo 1944 m. balandžio 15 dieną
pabėgo 11 „degintojų brigados" narių.

Here was the start of the underground
passageway used by 11 members of the so-called
burners' brigade to escape on 15 April 1944.

Returning to Vilnius we found that there were a few exceptions, and that not all Lithuanians were so barbaric. There is a church where the priest had realized what was happening, and travelled the shtetls to save their Torah. In all he collected 324 Torah's and hid them in the crypts of his Catholic Church. After the war, 300 of these were transferred to Israel, and 24 kept for Lithuanian archives and museums to teach what had happened. The same priest hid 2 families behind a false barrier in the study of his home. Their only respite was to be allowed out at night into a courtyard for some fresh air, to do what they had to do, eat, and go back. What was most extraordinary was that in the building across the courtyard were housed German soldiers. This went on for 18 months and both families survived, ultimately moving to Israel and the United States. The priest is memorialized at Yad Vashem as a Righteous Gentile.

We went to a large building complex that had housed poor Jews. The Nazis exterminated most very soon. But to save many, a Lithuanian 'Oscar Schindler', developed a motor vehicle repair factory and saved hundreds for nearly 2 years. Some got away. But even here the evil of the Nazis had its way. One day the workers were taken to another site to work. When they came back in the evening they discovered their children had been removed during the day, and killed at Paneriai. Two weeks before the Germans fled Vilna, they killed the rest.

Evidence of the richness of Jewish culture before the war is still present, even if it takes some imagination to conjure what it was. There is the large music school where Yasha Heifetz learned to play the violin, art communities, sites of Jewish schools, the Bohemian centers, the balcony from where Chaim Weitzman preached Zionism to the crowds, and so forth.

Finally, there are two reassuring signs. The first is the gradual resurgence of the Jewish community. Although now only 3000 compared to the prewar 75000, there is a Chabad Center and also an active Synagogue. We visited the Jewish Community Center and offices of the Jewish community official councils. A triumphant demonstration of survival for example is the fact that the Zadikoff Choir from Israel will sing in concert in Vilnius this Sunday night, September 7.

The other is the active approach of the current Lithuanian Government to make its people aware of the horrendous crimes committed between 1941 and 1944. There are the compulsory school programs, the monuments and signs and symbols around the city and countryside indicating what happened, the Holocaust and Jewish Museums, but above all, there are clear statements in many of these monuments that the atrocities were most often carried out by Lithuanians themselves, and only sometimes aided and abetted by the Germans.

This Utian family odyssey is not complete. Tomorrow Gordon and I go back to the archives to dig further. There are still many loose ends to explain. It is truly sad that we did not know what questions to ask our parents while they lived, and now we can only depend on documents to try and find answers. The journey has been successful beyond belief in what we have learned, what we have seen and the bonding that has solidified among five Utian family members. The greatest achievement of the trip is that we are now so truly proud to all be labeled Litvaks.

FRIDAY, SEPTEMBER 5.
VILNIUS CONTINUED

The highlight of the day was attending a Shabbat service at the Choral Synagogue with Brett. The low point was visiting the KGB Museum/ Prison and Museum of Genocide Victims.

Gordon and I started the day with a repeat visit to Galina at the Lithuanian Archives. We received notarized copies of our fathers' birth certificates and entries in the birth registers, and chased up additional information.

During the day a remarkable piece of information came in from my sister and brother. Martin found a photo dated 1918 with words written under the photo in Yiddish stating. "Female workers breaking gravel for paving of Aliya Street." This was from Tel Aviv! On the back of the photo my father's sister Glika had written 'This is the group of girls where we worked making gravel - breaking the stones. I am sitting near the boy so you can see where I am". So it now transpires that this Glika had preceded my sister Glika in travelling to Israel by at least 50 years.

The other coincidence is that they were both born on February 11. Sadly, Glika senior apparently caught malaria in Israel and returned to Lithuania thinking she would get better treatment. She perished in the forest in 1941. So a Utian, probably inspired to be a Zionist by visits of the likes of Chaim Weitzman to Vilnius in the early 1900's, was an early pioneer in Israel.

WRITTEN UNDER THE PHOTO IN YIDDISH IS AS FOLLOWS:
"FEMALE WORKERS BREAKING GRAVEL FOR PAVING OF ALIYA STREET"
ON THE BACK OF THE PHOTO:
"THIS IS THE GROUPS OF GIRLS WHERE WE WORKED MAKING GRAVEL - BREAKING THE STONES. I AM SITTING NEAR THE BOY SO YOU CAN SEE WHERE I AM".

Leaving the archives, Gordon and I met the boys at the KGB Museum/Prison and Museum of Genocide victims. The horrific history of the first Russian occupation of Lithuania followed by the Germans taking over on June 22, 1941, and then the reoccupation in 1944 by the Russians is documented in pictures, videos and so forth in the actual interrogation rooms. Most bone chilling is a walk through the cells and torture rooms in the basement. The execution room has running video of victims being dragged in by the KGB and shot in the back of the head.

The Jewish Genocide is also documented and a list of 1300 Righteous Gentiles from Yad Vashem tells of heroic efforts by some Lithuanians to save Jews from extermination.

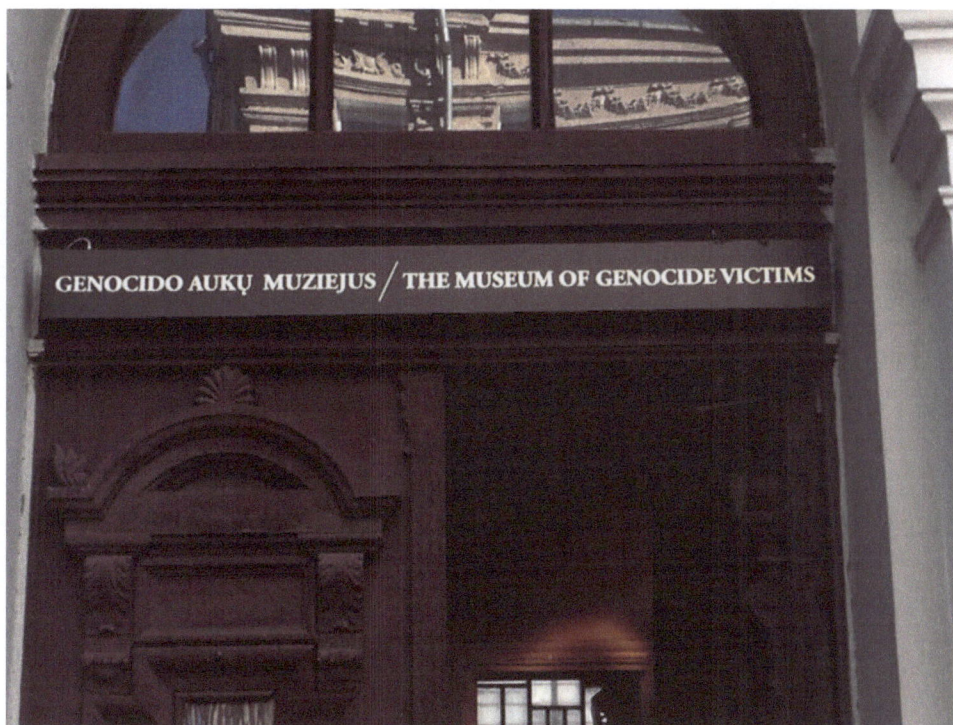

THE ENTRY TO THE KGB MUSEUM,
AND MUSEUM OF GENOCIDE VICTIMS

Taip dirbo ir degintojai, ir Ypatingoji komisija.
This is how the Burners' Brigade as well as the Special Commission operated.

Morduch Zaidel (1925–2008) escaped from the Vilnius Ghetto in 1943, but was caught, and in October sent to Paneriai to burn corpses. He escaped with the other members of the brigade and joined the partisans. After the war he lived in Israel.

Morduch Zaidel's testimony At first, in Paneriai we sawed firewood and built a bunker in the pits made for storing cisterns. We lived in the bunker, and there was a separate section for a kitchen and sleeping quarters. The pit was from four to four and a half metres deep, and we descended to it by a staircase. The Germans forced us to excavate the bodies of the victims and to carry them to the fires. We worked in shackles to prevent us from escaping.
Most of the victims were murdered by shots to the back of the head using the so-called dum-dum bullets. Children were undressed as were adults. Seventy percent of them were murdered by smashing their heads against a tree to save bullets. Often the victims were murdered like this: the murderers held the legs of the children and smashed their heads with the butt of a gun. Most of the victims had their hands tied and they were blindfolded with towels. All in all we excavated eight pits and burnt more than 68,000 bodies.
When prisoners of war arrived from the concentration camp, that is another nine people, we began to dig an underground tunnel under one of the walls. We got down to two metres 20 centimetres and dug a thirty-metre-long tunnel ... At 9:30 pm on 15 April 1944, we escaped by that tunnel to the partisans. Eleven of us escaped.

THIS IS HOW THE NAZIS TRIED TO HIDE THEIR ATROCITIES AT PANERIAI

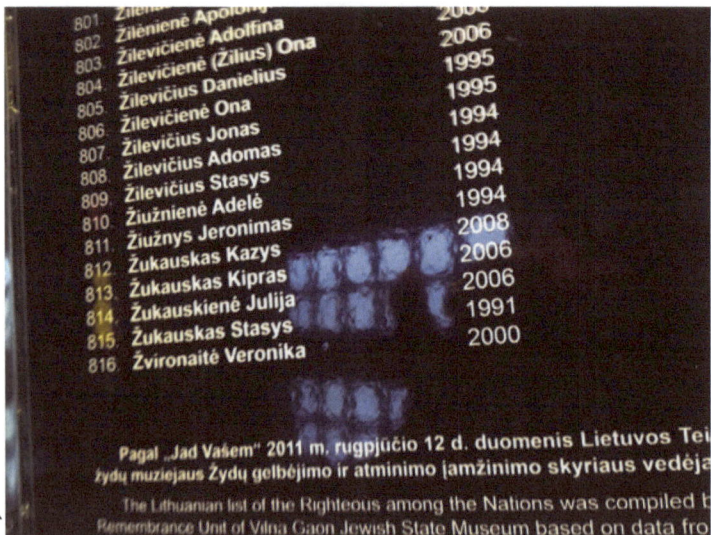

801.	Žilėnienė Apolonija	2006
802.	Žilėnienė Adolfina	2006
803.	Žilevičienė (Žilius) Ona	1995
804.	Žilevičius Danielius	1995
805.	Žilevičienė Ona	1994
806.	Žilevičius Jonas	1994
807.	Žilevičius Adomas	1994
808.	Žilevičius Stasys	1994
809.	Žiužnienė Adelė	2008
810.	Žiužnys Jeronimas	2006
811.	Žukauskas Kazys	2006
812.	Žukauskas Kipras	2006
813.	Žukauskienė Julija	1991
814.	Žukauskas Stasys	2000
815.	Žironaitė Veronika	
816.		

Pagal „Jad Vašem" 2011 m. rugpjūčio 12 d. duomenis Lietuvos Tei
žydų muziejaus Žydų gelbėjimo ir atminimo įamžinimo skyriaus vedėja

The Lithuanian list of the Righteous among the Nations was compiled b
Remembrance Unit of Vilna Gaon Jewish State Museum based on data fro

...AND THESE ARE SOME OF THE RIGHTEOUS GENTILES WHO TRIED THEIR BEST, AT RISK TO THEIR OWN LIVES

Getting out of that depressing place into the fresh air was a relief. Brett and I then wandered the city. It is a major holiday weekend, and the main street was closed for a miles-long street fair with vendors of everything possible along the way, marching military bands, and bandstands with music that extended late into the night. Along the way, on the main street in the middle of the activity we came a cross a Jewish musician playing Hava Nagilla on the clarinet. Further evidence of a Jewish presence was a poster displayed around town of the upcoming Sunday concert by the Zadikoff Choir of Israel. The Jews are back!!

Zadikoff Choir
From Israel

The most famous Israeli choir
is honored to invite
The Jewish Community of Vilnius
and its
Distinguished Friends and Guests
to enjoy a special and unique concert
celebrating
105 Years of Tradition, Music and Culture

Rich Repertoire
Jewish and Popular Israeli Songs

Conductor: Maestro Daniel Blank

The concert will take place on
Sunday, September 07, 6 PM
The Jewish Community of Lithuania
Pylimo str. 4
Vilnius

We look forward to seeing you soon!

AN ISRAELI CHOIR SINGS IN VILNIUS

Seventeen men, the Rabbi and his wife, attended Shabbat service at the Choral Synagogue, and Brett and I were the youngest. The service was touching. Just imagine the feeling of two generations of Utians returning to shul in Vilnius after an absence of over 70 years. The Rabbi conducted the entire service. His chanting was melodic, warm, sad, and incredibly well amplified by the design of the shul. The men were friendly and curious, smiling broadly when we explained we were Litvaks, but none of them spoke much English. One elderly man, who resembled my late father and his brother, told us he was the only member of his family to survive the Vilna Jewish Ghetto.

After services Brett and I went alone to dinner at a restaurant, the food here being exceptionally good, and reflected on our unique experience of the week. On the way home we walked into a rock concert on the square outside our hotel. The scene of well over a thousand attractive young people enjoying the music in a totally well behaved manner confirmed our opinion that something unique has happened in Lithuania since their gaining independence from the Russians in 1991. Vilnius is an undiscovered pearl of Europe, the total opposite of what any of us had anticipated. This has been a week of real contrasts.

Sadly Brett leaves for home tomorrow, as do I very early Sunday morning. This odyssey is ending, but all of us will leave inspired to continue trying to fill in some of the missing pieces.

TWO GENERATIONS OF
UTIANS ATTEND
SHABBAT SERVICE
AT THE CHORAL
SYNAGOGUE, VILNIUS

SATURDAY, SEPTEMBER 6.
TRYING TO TIE IT ALL TOGETHER

A FINAL GATHERING AT THE HOTEL,
AND BRETT DEPARTS FOR SOUTH AFRICA

As I hugged Brett in front of the hotel and watched him depart in his transport to the airport and South Africa, knowing I would not see him for months until Moira and I again went back to South Africa, I could not help but wonder what my grandfather Shmuel Mordechai must have thought and felt as he saw his sons leave for places unknown, fearing, unfortunately quite correctly, that he might never see them again.

While an overwhelming amount of information, new discoveries, and questions, are fresh in my mind, I take this moment to summarize my thoughts.

WHAT I DO KNOW

1. In the pre-war Lithuania of the 1930's, a shtetl was not necessarily just a grouping of wooden shacks with people living in poverty and Tevya wishing to be rich. Pasval, as an illuminating example, was a vibrant, thriving and active village with an educated community and a rich Jewish heritage. People were engaged in trades, commerce, the arts, and the professions, much as we are today in the places where we live.

2. The Jewish community, as now, had its religious observers and its secular Jews, many of whom were Zionists. My aunt Glika is an example, a Zionist who went to Israel in 1918 to help establish a Jewish homeland, and who might have lived a full life there had she not been infected with malaria and returned to Lithuania for presumed better medical care. Over 70% of Pasval Jews were registered as secular Zionists.

3. The original family name of our forebears was Utian. I always believed the name was abbreviated when my father, not speaking English, tried to explain it to a border control bureaucrat as he entered South Africa. But his birth record in the original birth register of 1905, of which I now have a certified copy, reads Utiansky and is then deleted and corrected to Utian.

4. The best theory I could be given by several of the people I spoke with is that Shmuel changed his name from Utian to Utiansky (Utianski) because it sounded more Lithuanian. Perhaps that was good for business.

5. My grandfather, Shmuel Mordechai Utiansky, was a successful businessman, engaged in the timber industry and fuel production. His second wife was a businessperson in her own right, and ran the only hotel in Pasval. They had the third telephone installed in Pasval, Number 3

6.   Changed fire codes around the central market area of Pasval in 1921/2 required that the wooden houses be replaced with brick structures. Harry and Boris must have been born in an original wooden structure, but soon after Harry left in 1920, the new residence/business was built. The family built the new house as both a place to live and work, incorporating the timber business office and the hotel. Unfortunately the brothers never seemed to be aware of this, hence Harry always leading us to believe the family continued to live in a wooden house.

7.   The 3 story house still stands, is an extremely attractive property, and has a bar and restaurant on the ground floor that gave 5 Utians the opportunity to drink a toast to all who had lived there, closing the circle.

8.   Shmuel Mordechai had ample resources to pay for Glika to travel to Israel and back, and Zelik and Beila, if not others, attained higher education and professional degrees.

9.   There was limited communication between Shmuel Mordechai and his son Abraham with Harry in South Africa, the most evidence uncovered thus far being a congratulatory letter from them to Harry wishing him and my mother well on the occasion of their wedding. Abraham wrote in English! Shmuel wrote in Yiddish. So Harry clearly had written to them that year to inform them of his upcoming marriage.

10.   Lithuania has a turbulent history with cycles of occupation, liberation and occupation. Until at least the mid 1930's the Jewish community in Lithuanian towns like Pasval lived a relatively peaceful symbiotic relationship with gentiles. The Germans acting as tourists around 1937-39 spread virulent anti-Semitism while people were under the cruel thumb of Russia, smearing the Jews as Bolshevik supporters of the Russians.

11.   The Germans occupied Lithuania and passed through Pasval for barely a few hours on June 26, 1941. They told people they had been liberated and that the Jews were Bolshevists who had collaborated with the Russians. Pasval non-Jewish citizens were told it was retribution time, and they could take anything belonging to Jews, so long as they got rid of them. The Pasval Town Council voted for extermination of the Jewish population, and local Lithuanians undertook this within weeks of the Germans giving them the go-ahead. The Jews were taken deep into a forest at Zadeikiuose, shot, and buried in a mass grave. It seems that few escaped.

12. Death registers confirm that many Utians were buried in the Jewish cemetery of Vilna from the late 1700's onwards. The state of the cemeteries makes any confirmation impossible. The same situation pertains to the Jewish cemetery in Pasval.

WHAT I DO NOT KNOW

1. Did Shmuel Mordechai's money and influence make the trip for Boris and Harry to London more straightforward than we have always believed? There is no way of answering this question. Otherwise, how did a 16-year-old travel alone from Pasval to London? What route did he take, what form of transport, how long was the journey, were there any nasty experiences along the way? And why did they leave? If relations between Jews and Gentiles were relatively calm, was the reason the potential conscription into the Russian Army, to get away from a stepmother, or to seek a better future in a new land?

2. Did any of the Utian/Utiansky family remaining in Lithuania have any sense of what was about to happen? How did Zelik and Beila get to Moscow, and become highly regarded professionals? Zelik became a Professor of Engineering at Moscow University and a member of the team that put sputnik in space. Beila was a pharmacologist.

3. Before 1938 what correspondence if any took place between the brothers in South Africa and the family in Pasval? Where and how did Abraham learn to read and write English?

4. Did any other of the Utian/Utiansky siblings get away before the end, and if so when and where did they go? Did any escape from the forest?

5. What made a relatively peaceful community turn into a revengeful bloodthirsty murderous mob in June-September of 1941? Was it jealousy of the Jewish community, simple greed to grab possessions, an antisemitic religious crusade, or what? They believed they had been liberated from the Russians. Within weeks of the extermination of the Jews they themselves found they were under the brutal thumb of the Nazis.

6. Was there any tie-in between the town of Utian (now Utena) and the Utian family? Coincidence is impossible, but we can find no birth or death records of Utians from Utian.

7. We know nothing about the family of our maternal grandmother Hesse Rochel nee Mozeson, who died on March 27, 1909, with my father less than age 4. What became of her siblings, and the rest of the Mozeson family?

8. Why did Boris and Harry choose to go to South Africa? Records from the Jewish Shelter on Leman Street in London, where Harry stayed before moving on, show that others went to the United States, Argentina, and Cuba.

FINAL THOUGHTS

As I finalize this document on Copenhagen Airport, awaiting my connection to Newark and home, I feel totally exhausted, yet I am thrilled and exhilarated. I came to Lithuania with low expectations of finding much, perhaps of confirming the existence of a poor family in a tiny shtetl.

Because of the reticence of my father to speak of the past, I had grown up with knowledge that we once had family in a place called Pasval in a country called Lithuania. But in my mind these people had been phantoms, never real with faces or ways I could relate them to aspects of living a real life.

But now I have walked where they walked, seen the same view from the window they would have seen, entered the family home and had a vodka in their memory, and tasted the flavor of a real town and a real place. I leave rapturous with the knowledge that I was completely wrong. I now relate in my mind to real people who really lived. All my perceptions of the past were figments of a young boy's imagination carried into my senior years, never corrected by a father who did not speak about his early life. My grandparents were people of stature in a town that was vibrant in its daily and community life. There are records of this in public documents in Vilnius and Pasvalys. Their children that remained in Pasval were able to be educated, and to travel. Shmuel Mordechai, with telephone number 3, must have been a pillar of his community.

I also leave Pasval and Lithuania horrified in the way this all ended. As much as I learned of the people and historic events, and looked at the killing fields, I could not get my mind around the enormity of this atrocity. Why?

WULF UTIAN,
PASVAL, LITHUANIA, SUNDAY, SEPTEMBER 7, 2014
CLEVELAND, OHIO, USA, WEDNESDAY, OCTOBER 8, 2014